The Sun Rises as Does the Moon

The Sun Rises as Does the Moon

poems by
Judith Heilizer

Minneapolis

Second Edition December 2022
The Sun Rises as Does the Moon
Copyright 2021 Judith Heilizer
All rights reserved.

10 9 8 7 6 5 4 3 2

ISBN 978-1-960250-18-6

Cover design: Gary Lindberg
Book layout & design: Christopher Chambers

This writing is dedicated to my children and to the people they love. —J. H.

Contents

1. The World

The Rake and the Garden..........2
Savior..........4
The Sun Rises as Does the Moon..........6
The Air Around Us..........8
New Year's Eve..........9
The Cold..........10
Lecture..........12
All There Is..........14
On a Bus in Washington DC, Summer 1952..........16
Everyone and Everything..........18
After Selling the Summer Place..........21
Grace..........24
Choices..........26
Thanksgiving..........28

11. Grief

The Colors and Sounds of Love..........32
On My Birthday..........33
Support Group..........34
Grief..........36
Obituaries..........38
Tears..........40
Lenten Rose..........41
Sadness..........42
Colorforms..........44

Observations.........45
Intensive Care Unit.........46
Elegy in Two Parts.........48
Toby.........51

11. Spirit

After the Concert.........54
The Dragonfly's Wings.........55
Kaddish.........56
Darkness and Light.........59
Shapeless and Precious Days.........62
A Kind of Love.........64
Meditation.........65
Yesterday's Perfume.........66
Seven Kinds of Love.........68
Til Death Do Us Part.........70
In the Mirror.........72

1. The World

The Rake and the Garden

There is a corner in the back of my garden where
unwanted things go like the cracked glazed pot I used to treasure
and now hardly remember
and my kid's rake from when he was four
I offered it to his kids but they did not want it
and I realized that I had saved it because
I knew one day my son would leave

amidst all that stuff in the corner of my garden
lies a little decaying wooden box
and though I rarely go there I am drawn to look into it and I do
it is filled with rainwater from this morning's shower
and in the rainwater floats a bumble bee
its wings spread out waiting
without struggle or despair, no sense that it has given up
just a quiet being with whatever is now

not able to let things be I cautiously pour out the water
and the bee, which shakes itself and then takes off in flight
though I am not sure it matters
this too is as it should be

I rake my garden and the matted leaves peel off willingly
having done their job protecting the creatures and plantings
through the winter, nourishing what is to come

suddenly I hear the soft insistent wail of a tiny creature
its nest laid bare by my rake

it crawls over the edge of the nest to find itself

in an unknown space a baby mouse maybe
I do not really look
instinctively I reach out and encircle its warm wriggling body
I place it back into the nest with its siblings
spread the soft mound of fur, their mother's, and the matted leaves
back over the nest just as I had found it almost

but every day I peek and the more often I do
the less agitation happens in the nest
and I am glad of it

one day it dawns on me that these little mice
have ceased looking like mice
and have turned into baby rabbits and
though I am not sure it matters
this too is as it should be

the wise mother made her nest near my vegetable garden
knowing how well they will be fed and how safe
they are in this surround

I see again that everyone and everything in the universe are connected
that what happens to one happens to us all
that when we protect others we protect ourselves
that when we heal others we heal ourselves
this is Tikkum Olam
this is the promise of love embracing the world

Savior

I would never have noticed
this bug on its back except for
the rhythmical movement of the silkthread legs

a dying maneuver practiced for millions of years

I am a newcomer and see the world through
the tiny perceptions of my incarcerated mind
drawing conclusions which wipe out past knowings

and so I flip the bug onto its belly
self indulgent and satisfied by my kindness

within a moment so brief
as though it had never been
the bug flips itself onto its back

its legs take up their dance
I flip it back over
and it flips itself over again

I say to the bug
don't you get it I am here to save you

in the morning I return
and the legs are still moving
you must be tired I think
too tired not to allow me to save you
so I can feel good

don't you know that life needs to be lived
and death should be thwarted at every opportunity

then again it happens between us
as it had every time before
I do, the bug undoes

I go through my day avoiding the bug
and when I visit that night
the little legs are still
folded perfectly across its chest

when I return later
there is nothing there
except for some flakes of dust

Spirit, help us to know
just a little of what Your creatures know
of the goodness of being
and of not

leaving it
just as you made it
just as it is

The Sun Rises as Does the Moon

A strange time this, made up of opposites
too much time and fear of running out of time
too many warnings and too little trust
too much longing and not enough holding
too many memories and not enough echo

time is elastic, pulled this way and that
seemingly inexhaustible while the egg timer
ticks and ticks and ticks

warnings blare from electronic watchmen
shredding the silence

arms reach out to you and yours rise to meet them
taking a furtive inventory of mask and proximity
is the treasured other now a bearer of ruin?

the worst of it is that you cannot know
what is truth unless you know you cannot be safe
there is an ease that comes when all that is known
may no longer be

still the sun rises as does the moon
the land greens and browns and greens again
creatures chirp and mate and children giggle

we steal furtive glances at each other
searching for echo, for hope

and so it will come
some day

The Air Around Us

Have you noticed how the air around us
changes its color and its shape?

how it sparkles with the silvery laughter of children
how it curls tightly around what is wounded
how it sags into dull brown when lovers part
how it holds us warm and close when we are happy
how it glitters like the sharp edge of a knife when we spar
how it shrinks darkly into itself when we lose what we need
how it hides when it all is too much?

on the sidewalk a grey-haired couple lumbers through
the grey air that surrounds them
leaning this way and that as they bump into each other
apologies no longer required
his arm moves out and curls protectively around her waist
she accepts his gesture without acknowledging him
an instinctive habit of love and time
the grey air around them turns a gossamer rose
trembles ever so briefly with possibility

when his arm drops from the effort
they plod ahead just as before
and the blush-tinged air folds back
into the place where these things live
in the greyness of the now.

New Year's Eve

Though his back blocks my view of her
it seems as though he strokes her shoulders gently
as he takes her coat
then gestures to her with a smile
to seat herself at the table opposite him

it is the stillness in his face as he looks at her
in the quiet that comes of a perfect match
needing nothing other than what is

it is the shimmer of his love
in the space between them
in which he holds her

the briefest interruption posed by menu choices
she will have this, I will have that, thank you
his words floating outside the gossamer web
of their togetherness

after dinner he rises, folds her coat carefully
around her and guides her by the elbow to the door

I look after them wanting to be knowing her
wanting her to be loving him
There is no one with him

it has been ten years already?
She was such a wonderful woman...

Judith Heilizer | *The Sun Rises as Does the Moon*

The Cold

The youngest cashier at Trader Joe's
stationed near the door in December
responds to my asking if he feels chilly
without a sweatshirt
No I can take it I'm from Wisconsin

in 1944 in the frozen woods of Poland
mothers hold out their children beseeching
their captors to shoot them quickly
freezing to death is painful

today ducks give up their down
and other creatures their pelts
not willingly but we are smarter and bigger and stronger
so we take what we want
we kill deer for the sport of it
when the cold drives them into the open
to search for food and for water
and we call it harvesting to make it sound all right
like calling lampshades made of human skin art

in 1944 from wells cleared briefly of typhoid infected corpses
thrown in to speed the spread of death
we drew water into buckets in the dead of night
poured it into a bathtub where it froze
to be chipped off in bits and sucked to relieve thirst
and occasionally melted for washing of sorts

today fires rage in Aleppo
the hoses that would bring water
are frozen in hatred

in 1944 a few twigs burning in a stovepipe to warm
a potato and a turnip and maybe a tulip bulb
then rolled them into a blanket for hours
to finish cooking them sort of

today I pass a man shoveling snow in the icy cold
I say hello, and say it's almost May.
He thanks me as though I'd given him a gift

this is how easy it can be sometimes
just saying yes, I know it is cold
but it can change some day

Lecture

I find it hard to decide
who is me and who is the distorted
reductio absurdum of me

I am introduced with a certain amount of fanfare
to students who need the credits my talk offers them
part of their education requirement or whatever

I watch myself standing calm and resolute
telling difficult tales of war and destruction
offering insights which presumably will lead to reason
and hopefully to deterence at a later unknowable moment

In truth I am a purveyor of the unimaginable
distilling it to fluid elegant sentences
toneless dirges set to music

while I speak I experience sudden squalls of fright
I hear my story describing a sepia faded photograph
which I airbrush to give it relevance and substance
I see myself borrowing from the pain of others and my own
I sense that I am speaking from the inside of mirrors patinaed
by time and rendered indistinct and interchangeable

threatened by paralysis or worse surrender sometimes
my mind crawls into the audience and watches myself
listen to myself an odd and calculating and necessary
quality control on the truth or so it seems

but this never helps to dispel the surreality
of trying to rehydrate dessicated slivers of presence

I wind up my lecture with thoughtful cheerful conclusions
a kind of take-home prize for their attendance
the students burst into a standing ovation and
I am caught in the glare of the light
and all I can do is cry.

All There Is

This is about the tiny black dot
moving in a straight line
on my white windowsill
the smallest speck imaginable
just a blink away from invisibility
had I breathed a bit closer
I would have blown it away

I carefully place my fingertip into its path
the tiny black dot stops a small distance away
leaving just enough space around my finger
and then moves on

I am uneasy, apologetic
I had not meant for it to be a scientific experiment
it has eyes I think and maybe ears and also legs
it has children and it makes decisions
and it lives by the consequences
and maybe it is immortal in one shape or another
I can't fathom that because I am not

I wonder what its purpose is
could it be perhaps that on its shoulders
the Universe balances
how am I to know

but then
I am not willing to take the risk of finding out
by doing away with it

with an imperceptible sigh
or a wipe of my sponge

so tell me little one
did you come to teach me
that power is not an aggregate of size
that each bit of the universe contains all of the universe

am I to learn
that this infinite universe is balanced
on the tiniest welcoming smile
the most imperceptible opening of the heart
the smallest gesture of care for others
the barely visible gift of love

if this is your lesson
then let there be gratitude
for you are taking a chance for all of us
calling us to you
trusting that we will hear your message
trusting us with all there is

On a Bus in Washington DC, Summer 1952

Waiting for a bus she seems a bit older than I,
though not by much or maybe not at all
given that experience is not measured in parametric mathematics
that selves shaped by rules that serve only the rule maker
grow lopsided

she is of saturated ebony and eyes the color of liquid lava
and of rebellious pitch-black wiry hair
while I of faintly blushed Northern descent
have eyes of seaglass and masses of complaint curls
more so she has what I yearn for
a large round belly, her baby due soon

the overheated asphalt vomits its foul breath
on her and on me in equal measure
as we climb into the air-cooled bus
my hand inviting or heaven forbid
inducing her to go first

there is one seat open in the front of the bus
I motion for her to sit while she shakes her head no
our eyes lock then tear apart
and neither of us takes the seat

the passengers' frozen stares morph eerily into
a wordless hiss I hear as murmured disdain
the hiss of gas
spewing from the gas chamber's faucet

in the slave labor camp mother and daughter
each save their daily ration of soup for the other
at roll call they brush past each other barely alive

their eyes lock then tear apart
they pour the soup onto the ground
neither will take what the other can't lose
the seat on the bus remains empty

Everyone and Everything

They were all children
like yours and mine

they were anticipated with delight
or dreaded for their neediness
or at worst thought irrelevant
they were seen and known and loved
or not

these children created the world in their own image
through the eyes of their parents and their teachers
who taught them who they were
and what was true and right
and what was false and wrong

and because they were children
they needed to trust those truths and make them their own
so they could feel safe and not alone
and without love

now these particular children
learned from the adults whose love they needed
about the pleasures of anger and power
and what they can accomplish from these adults
who had been children once upon a time

now there is a sadness and they hurt all the time
because they have learned that what you feel
is not what you are told to feel

and that you must listen to what you are told
so that you can be loved

now this anger makes them feel powerful
and it buries their hurt

so they learn to dismiss the Other
if they are less then you are more
and so it makes you strong
and makes everything you do right
even if it does not feel that way

the taste of hatred lies bitter on the tongue

and the hurt goes deep inside
into an empty chasm
where the Other becomes a thing
to be used, erased, rendered nonexistent

in places like Auschwiz and Pittsburgh
and in teepees and holy places and gay bars
and in slave quarters and in cages of children
and during traffic stops

what they do not know
because they have not been told
is that love and joy and delight and surprise
are also the victims of this bleak hatred
in which the Other ceases to exist

and so these children themselves perish
from lack of love
this is how it works
but understanding is not excusing or forgiving

so let us hold dear
the things we tell our children
the things we show our children
the things we teach our children to believe
the things we charge our children to do
the things we are

for our children are our power
and our executors

and if we do not do these things
our children will become
our executioners

for they will not have souls
to keep them whole

let us give our children
love and trust and happy anticipation
in who they can become and how they can glow
in the perfect circle of every one and every thing
in this beautiful world

After Selling the Summer Place

after the sorting and the packing
I walk to the enchanted tree house
adolescent giggles entice me to open the door
but no one is there
just the cots stacked neatly in the corner
folding chairs covered with dust

I close the door hoping to capture their voices
inside this magical place
so whoever will be here next will hear them
and smile and wonder

the old charred wood and ash in the firepit are covered in moss
the pond so still it reflects the beauty of the fall maples
swimming in rapturous color

I see the littles ones' wiggly brown bodies splashing
naked making mudpies while the older ones
stare at their painted toenails, languidly flip their hair
or make muscles and compare the bulges in their speedos
giggling about secrets they hope are risqué
and exuberant dogs and hopping toads flipping up the sand

the sand pile is undisturbed and the chairs are gone

I walk up the hill where raspberries and flowers
spent by autumn prepare for next spring

the front sunroom like the rest of the house is empty

but I see tables set in Thanksgiving hues
the scents of food and the joy of abundance
the noise and the tiny tug of worry
will we all be here again next year? please?

and the kitchen cluttered with stuff and smells
and people and labor and laughter
and occasional crabbiness
now empty

upstairs in the bedrooms fireplaces are ready to warm the air
and the echo of marital whispers remains
shshsh the kids will hear us
the guest bedroom is emptied of its cribs and diapers
a box of tampons in the bathroom

downstairs in the empty playroom vacant shelves once stocked
with books and games and knitting projects
a squirrel skeleton and crayons and paper and paint
beads and gifts made of tongue depressors
cots for sleepovers with friends

and a quiet spot for time outs

I do not feel alone here which would suggest a loss of connection,
on the contrary connections pull me here and there and everywhere
with dizzying speed into complexity and richness

I can touch life and fullness and joy and love so vividly
that I am not entirely sure where I am here in this moment
or in my memories

but I do feel a sense of incompleteness
that something is missing
an awareness of absence
and I pause on the porch to let go of my aloneness
while I listen for the sounds of my family

I search for a refuge from this longing for the past
struggle with my awareness that all moments become pasts
as soon as they are born
I try to understand that each is already irretrievably lost
to the fleeting presence of the next

but I do know that state of solitude in which memories flourish
a way of being which shimmers with joy and with forgiveness
taking me to the acceptance and peace that comes
from claiming all of what was and all of what is to be

I close the door behind me one last time.

Grace

Moments before the store closes I run in
the young man with a broom
looks at me kindly
his face tranquil
without a hint of resentment at this intrusion
into his freedom so near at hand

I ask where to find the ribbon I am looking for
he responds with unhurried care
making sure I will find my way
then he turns back to his sweeping

I am briefly arrested by his acceptance and obliging
I taste the pleasure of being seen and known
in this fleeting moment that almost wasn't

he meets me at the checkout counter
neither of us has waited for the other
and the feeling of grace persists
in this tiny speck of time

I pay and he wraps my little purchase
then slides the receipt across the counter
for my signature

and I see that the arm with which he moves the paper
ends above where his elbow should have been
the skin there hardened and smoothed by use

I am shaken as the world tumbles between
what I expected and what I see

I try to remain impassive while I wonder
why he does not use his other hand
until I see that it too is compromised
two fingers and nothing more

the silence between us is shocking in its ordinariness
I sign the receipt and thank him and take my package
we look at each other ever so briefly and smile
acknowledging the journey everyone takes who meets him
the pain assumed for him and experience for ourselves

I think about my children and their perfect limbs
my sister a compassionate physician who
to help lessen the distress of a difficult pregnancy
had sent me samples of thalidomide
which I flushed down the toilet not knowing anything

before I leave I turn to wish him a pleasant evening
he has come away from the register and resumed his sweeping
he stands in the aisle with the broom in one half-fingered hand
and I see his leg, a steel rod protruding from shorts
ending in a sneaker attached to it in some mechanical way
the other leg a black metal and mesh cage ending in the other sneaker

I smile at him and he smiles back
the air shimmers
with the grace of compassion
setting us both free

Choices

An ordinary summer evening if there is such a thing
near closing time at the garden center
and a huge space fenced and gated where I seem to be alone
among row after row of shelves of potted plants
one narrow exit leading to the lit and busy space of the store

I'm admiring the hostas when I see a head hovering
above the shelves a short distance away
dark skin and curly dark hair and brown eyes turned inward

my stomach tightens
I measure the distance between me and the exit
while the man floats between

I hear my father's voice saying:
child, the worst sin of all is prejudging
it leads to all the unspeakable pain this world holds
the best is love
practice love

I move on unshackled then
suddenly I feel a touch
a stroking lighter than the touch of down
the brush of a dragonfly's wing
moving from my ear down my neck to my shoulder blade

I whirl trying to find my center
the figure has already slid on soundlessly

an anxious woman's voice cuts the silence:
"Joe, No, we don't touch people, Joe come here right now"
she runs toward me apologizing

I turn, incredulous at her anxiety
and find myself saying that it is all right, it's really all right
that is the gentlest I've been touched all day
I cherish it

her voice breaks and tears well
"oh" she breathes, "you understand"

I stand quietly waiting not knowing what there is to understand
Joe has slid between us looking out from the uncluttered space
of his autism, his eyes here and there and elsewhere
our disparate worlds woven together by the gossamer thread
of innocence distilled into a touch

I watch myself turning toward him and taking his hands in mine
he does not move

I introduce myself and I tell him I'm happy to have met him
and I thank him

his eyes look through and past me
he is very still, the air between us shimmers
and I want to stay in this space for a long long time

Thanksgiving

Fall scents rising from crumbling leaves awaken me
to insistent ancient whispers that winter is coming
and with it hunger and cold
I want to cook soup and bake pies

beans and onions and carrots and squash
pumpkins and sweet potatoes dive into my cart
with the nuts and spices and brown sugar
the extroverted colors of fall

the woman in line behind me has only three items in her cart
I smile and gesture her ahead of me
she smiles, in thanks and comments
on the beauty of the bounty in my cart
I compliment the color of her sweater

when it is my turn I put my groceries on the belt
minding the order in which I will want to unpack them
watch them slide through the checker's hands

she smiles and says how are you and thank you
and I say fine and thank you and have a nice day
but I am elsewhere in my mind wondering
whether the frozen stuff will make it home if I run another errand

I also thank the baggers
while trying to remember where I parked my car
I notice her old hands, small and veiny
I look up to find her face and

I see my Mother's face

alabaster skin scored by age
grey streaked hair held in a bun

tears that have lain in wait well up and run down
the inside of my heart

"thank you," I say, "thank you"
though I am not sure to whom I am speaking

the woman's eyelids flutter briefly

I go home to make soup and pie.

II. Grief

The Colors and the Sounds of Love

A sliver of silver
dances soundlessly
on the deep blue waves of memory
a sparkle of lavender
the nearness of the beloved

delicate hues these
not the browns and yellows and oranges
rumbling with volume of the now

nor are they the dark sounds and colors
of being or of ceasing to be
nor of the emperor virus
shaking us to remember how it was before

these are the memories
of the translucent being
of the other traveling our orbit
silenced now

the brain begs for affiliation
rakes our memories for soothing
nothing comes

there is no substitute
for the colors and the sounds
of love

On My Birthday

I would like to know who my mother was then
Was she lying on her bed, moaning in anguish
or perhaps in pleasure
as she pushed me away from her?

Had she moaned in anguish or in pleasure nine months earlier?
Had she pushed him away also, perhaps too soon or not soon enough?

A clothesline of memories, wrinkled or fuzzy, or smooth edged
waving in the breeze.
A basketful more, some folded,
others bunched or worn thin, still waiting to be hung.

I pass by the shriveling face in the mirror, the indulgent rage
at shrinking looks and time and chances
the raucous emptiness of things unsaid and undone.

Children are so forgiving it aches
Do you not see how I have failed you?
Please, blame me. I blame myself.

Then, dawning into the here and now
the simplicity of gratitude

Then after the blaming, send me your clemency
and your mercy

Support Group

The magnetized mantra sorry for your loss
holds this group together, our own loss
resonating with the losses of others
like tuning forks promising the easing
of grief by the sharing of it

don't you know that it is not my loss
that I did not participate in the loosing,
that it was foisted upon me against my will
without my agreement, against my opposition?

after my turn I accept thanks
with a half-humble smile
for my willingness
to open my soul for inspection

the pale skeleton of my grieving
picked bare of any semblance of flesh or feeling,
the anatomy lesson of absence
called sharing your journey

when I fall silent
a flat dark shadow slides over the gurney
the sheet of mercy when all else has failed to be of
meaning or understanding

after the polite stillness
a cycle of buzzwords meant to empathize
soothe, heal, finally let go

but that's just the point. I need to breathe
life into my grief. I need to hold it,
keep it close, just as it is
in the deep spiney darkness inside me
without meddling with its raucous rawness.

for it and I belong together
and neither of us can be
without the other

Grief

Sometimes I feel I am a person
knitted from memories
some of them of her shiny black bangs
rocking her crib
across the floor and wiggling
out of my hugs on her way to conquests
defiance and endless questioning
and doing and doing and
never feeling good enough and
then doing more and giving more
wife, parent, sister
A daughter offering up a brief sort of peace
even laughter, considering the absurdity
of our relationship in which we traded places
on a schedule neither of us understood
or cared to understand. It was just that way.

sometimes the emptiness in the wake
of her death grabs the loose thread
on the top of my head and plays with it
like a cat with a ball of yarn unraveling
me until I am a pile on the floor
memories and aching disbelief
tangled beyond
definition or recognition.

sometimes I touch the threadbare shawl
she always wore for security or luck
and I beg her to help me cry.

Then I feel around for my needles
and add more stitches,
busy myself with knitting
myself back into a shelter of memory

Obituaries

Every morning I visit the dead
with the morning paper
though I try to skip on to the crossword puzzle
they make me stop at their page first

I want to escape their grasp
I scan the pages without looking at them
eager to get to where I want to be

see us they say we deserve your attention
and I yield to them reluctantly

photographs of men in uniforms from long ago wars
fancily dressed debutantes carefully coiffed
smiling back at me
and photographs of their older selves smiling then by habit

I am as always startled not having thought of death
as a state of amusement or bemusement

the stories in the photographs vary in tone
and in length and in detail of their virtuous lives

nonetheless an eerily similar pattern of words
surrounds each photograph
a loving and beloved family member a doer of good
their passing soft and gentle more often than not
a battle valiantly fought

I wonder what I am to learn
perhaps it is just the knowledge that we all
will find a home on this page
one day

Tears

Have you noticed
how tears do not leave stains

they come unbidden or longed for
in droplets or in cascades

then they are gone
as if they had never been

they do not ask to be known
except in the crevices of the soul

stains are about marking
a calling attention to

stains insist on being seen and known
jogging memories of pain

stains change the landscape
leaving proof of what has been

until they fade through cleansing or time
by sleight of hand or by the sun

but tears do not leave stains

I wonder what I am to learn

Lenten Rose

I remember seeing the Lenten rose
blooming shyly
through the melting snow
in early spring

I gently caressed the petals
without touching them
except with my joy

until I dared the gauziest of touches

only then did I remember
how petals that emerge too early
will freeze and shatter
under the gentle touch
into shards of possibility perished

so it can be when one loves
and I did

You sent out delicate blooms
into the others' barely warming heart
you would not wait for the melting
not wanting to believe that it was not yet spring

your love's petals froze and shattered
untouched by joy
perishing in spring
before the warmth of summer love
could keep them safe

Sadness

I want to know more of sadness
its feel and sound and color and scent and taste

sadness has a velvety touch, almost welcoming
like the worn cushions on the antique rocker my son gave to me

a kind of softness
unlike the sharp shrill edges of despair which cause you to wail
and seek a hiding place far away from yourself
or the grasp of melancholy holding you captive in its limpid arms

sadness is the monotone sound of the gong as it recedes
forever into space
not the shrieking insistence of despair
or the gnawing sound of melancholy receding from your raw edges

sadness is dark green with little flecks of subdued possibility,
while despair flares in primary colors
grabbing your attention lest you forget
melancholy is the slow nondescript compounding of loss

sadness has a sort of cloying sweetness
inviting us to linger while knowing we must move on
while despair tastes harsh and bitter
and melancholy offends by its blandness, its lack of definition

the scent of sadness has a certain mildness
offers a bit of seduction, a hint of indulgence
while despair is sharply and cleanly odorless
and melancholy smells putrid and its breath clings

so if I must mourn
give me sadness for my companion
for its softness and quiet and hue
its sweet savor and gentle taste
on my way home.

Colorforms

We teach our little ones
about the world in shapes and colors and numbers
round and blue and pink and brown triangles
one and two and all they need to know

he shakes them out of their bottles
nine pills, sometimes eleven
different shapes and colors
oval and round and square or triangular
each of the soft hues of a gentle rainbow
rose and aqua and lavender
a determined red or yellow or green
and sometimes a plain white

at the appointed time
they go on their lifesaving missions
floating inward on a sip of water
the right kind in the right quantity in the right order
on a schedule dictated by purpose

sometimes though they quit their mission
without warning or knowable reason

then the search is on to find a replacement
to make do or for doing better

is this why I taught him about colors and shapes and numbers
when he was still little?

Observations

I was afraid
willing my car to speed over the wet leaves
following the ambulance to the Emergency Entrance
whirling red lights and sirens shredding the silence
in the darkness of the dying night
holding my empty self captive
birdsongs sticking in their throats

inside the curtained cubicle cheery beeps and humming
dancing displays obscure their purpose

time stumbles by
changing in color and consistency

footsteps come and pass and stop
voices cut through the fuzz of waiting

then release
as shy dawn light pushes the night back to its musty lair
and in the rearview mirror taillights bounce off the sign
receding behind me: Emergency Exit
my face insists that I exist
as the tires roll home over the sun-gilded leaves
and sweet birdcalls urge life to begin again

And so it is done
until the next time

Intensive Care Unit

After the busyness of the ambulance
there is the waiting room of the ICU
walls the color of steel or the beige of an empty canvas
on which to paint ones fears and hopes
chairs arranged around circular tables
or alone in a corner against a wall

your choice to share this thing or to hold it by yourself
or to travel back and forth depending upon the distance you need
from your tarry insides

I am motioned in from behind the glass door
how do they know to whom I belong?

the other side the hallway is also of steel and beige
interrupted by gurneys weighted and silent

at the end of the hall waits mine
his at least for this hovering stage
he is tethered by tubes that draw out death and drip in life
from bags filled with magic and saline
his face ironed flat and unrecognizable, glazed into stiffness
his eyes scanning nothing

the air is thick with echoes of past petitions demands groveling
weird unkeepable bargains chasing one another to nowhere
this air is without character heavy with the scent of desperation
it makes no demands and poses no challenges
and we breathe it like thick grey water

it is the motionlessness of it all, a wild war for life being waged
in silence recorded on charts with lines and numbers
an army of oddly-shaped forms that register and measure
and calculate and sound alarm

nasal tubes like small glistening rivers for oxygen
and for a colorless liquid called food doing the work of life

he is way too young to be so still
his eyes steep and empty like a well run dry
his right side lifeless then suddenly frenzied
kicking at a world that has failed him

so they shackle him to the gurney by his hands and his feet
for safety they say though they don't say for whose

my thoughts blow around like dryer fuzz
I cannot tell what is real and what is not
the emptiness vibrates with unaskable questions
that fill the space and spill out into the hallway
screaming in silence
why

and then
please oh please

Elegy in Two Parts

1.
He lies neatly on the narrow bed with side rails
and metal loops for restraints
washed and fed and diapered and medicated

so still that she watches for the rise and fall of his chest
before beginning her indictment

you left me standing alone in a life which needed us both
to be lived after promising before God that you would be here
in sickness and in health til death do us part

but you deserted me plain and simple
you left me standing alone without an explanation

I don't know where you went or what you were thinking
you just go on with your days and your nights
as though we were still together you and I

your leaving began so gradually I hardly knew it at first
an absentminded kiss, a forgotten date
you wearing a shirt you knew I hated
then you stopped noticing the little things about me you had loved
you eluded my attempts to draw you back into my conversation
my world

when I grew angry or when I cried you sat there
looking inward where I could not follow or be comforted by you
and you did not turn around to look for me
you never seemed to realize that I was not there

mostly you are silent now
or when you do speak I cannot hear an echo
sometimes you sing fragments of old songs we both love
but when I join in you stop
I am unwelcome in your melody

except that every once in a while you look at me and say
do you remember us in Paris walking together at night
over he bridge across the Seine and how the streetlights
poured silver shimmers over the ebony water?

how could you be so unfair?

sometimes I fasten my eyes onto yours
trying to hold them and force them to see
but they just fold inward and slip away

I search for you everywhere
as one searches for a forgotten melody
among notes from which one strings memories
to make having lost them bearable

I cannot find you anywhere
and I cannot stop looking for you.

2.
He waits until it is quiet then
opens his eyes briefly to make sure she is gone
after she has left he gets to play with his thoughts

he gets to bounce them around
what was up slides down
what was there disappears and something else
slips in to join the impromptu polonaise
of color and sound and motion

when he reaches out to touch the thoughts
they become powdery and drift away
assuring him of an ever changing show

he is the grand conductor
a master of sleight of thought

sometimes he tumbles into laughter and claps his hands
and they feed him more pills
so he has to rearrange his thoughts
coax them back to where they were before

he loves his world of magic and wants to invite others
to play with him and his dancing thoughts
but there is no one there to hear

when they come in for the midnight bed check
he draws the curtain across the stage
and pretends to be asleep

they note on his chart
patient quiet and sedated

after he is sure they have melted away
he takes his bow and draws the curtain.

Toby

My dog Toby came home today in a box
inside a white gift bag lined with blue tissue paper
a heart and his name drawn in marker
his collar at the bottom of the bag
still holding his scent

I wanted so much to speak to him
and so I did
I told him how I had failed him
by taking him from expert to expert
trying to make untrue what we had been told
a truth he had accepted as he always accepted truths
with a grace that I lacked

I told him that I'had needed to hold him
for a long time before
during and even after
the needle dripped peace
into his aching body
while my eyes held his eyes
unable to let them close
and his eyes held mine
until I could leave him

I told him
when I am ready
I will dig a hole
beneath the lilac bush
for you.

III. Spirit

After the Concert

At his kitchen table, two glasses of wine
his hand edging towards mine
stopping just short of touching
I wonder will I come here again?

I want to, I think

At my kitchen table, two glasses of juice
each of us reading:
he a medical journal, I a book of poems
our hands curled around our glasses.

At our kitchen table, two glasses of water
his hands in his pockets
asleep in his wheelchair
my hands on the computer keyboard

busy with other people's things.

The Dragonfly's Wings

I am afraid of not being able to remember
the luminescence of the dragonfly's wings in sunlight

of only being able to remember
how blind I was when the light faded

of not being able to remember glimmers
of light dancing on water

of only being able to remember darkness
because it is easier to remember than light

of not being able to remember that love becomes invisible
if we barter it only with those we deem deserving

of only being able to remember what I have received
shrinking my gifts to measure for measure

of remembering
and of not remembering

Spirit, please send me memory
of the dragonfly's wings shimmering in the sunlight.

Kaddish

We are walking home through the dark and sticky August night, my grandsons and I, the warmth of their hands, a moist mixture of comfort and sleepiness, snuggled into mine. Two and three years old they are, all motion and sound, and pulling and lagging and little steps dancing next to mine.

We pass through a familiar playground and the pitch-black night suddenly fills with possibility. They pull away, climb on walls and jump off, laughing, daring and trusting the night, because in their world the alternative is unimaginable.

They speak to themselves, to one another, to the sky, to what is invisible, to me. I get lost in their sounds. Sometimes they become insistent that I answer them even though I cannot understand most of their words, and I ask them to tell me again. And they do, patiently reframing and repairing until finally I can repeat a semblance of what they have said to me. They make do with my approximations and do not judge me for my limitations.

I tell them things too, about how good their hands feel in mine, about how much I love walking with them in this dark, dark night, how safe we are, and how much I love loving them.

The children have found their shadows. Magically, depending on where the streetlights are their shadows precede or follow them, shorten or lengthen them, fatten or thin them out. They jump on one another's shadows and together they jump on mine, exuberant in their conquest, secure in their invincibility.

Sometimes we each split into two, our bodies and our distorted shadow selves, each a faint and altered representation of who we are. And when we step into the circle of the street lights the shadows vanish and we are ourselves again, alive and whole and one.

I spin a cocoon of happiness around us and fill it with gratitude for their wisdoms and for my eyes to see.

But I feel an uneasiness, a tiny tear in my cocoon. At first I pay it no mind, But the tear widens and I know I cannot ignore it for fear I will plummet through if I don't watch out.

Darkness of another kind seeps into the crack of the cocoon, bleak and menacing, filled with tiny sounds hiding in an immense silence, the crack of dead night, knocking. The sounds of the voices of the children who walked trustingly hand in hand with their fathers and their mothers to their death. They were the voices of the children who asked: " Abba, Ima, Father, Mother, where is the burnt offering?" The sounds of their parents silence, powerless to stem their childrens' leap across the chasm of dawning, terrifying comprehension.

These children lived and died on macabre playgrounds of adults unlit by humanness,
where jumping off a wall meant jumping into an abyss, where losing was winning and living was losing.

These children also walked among shadows but these shadows were not of the children. These shadows did not vanish in the light. These shadows had thickness and cruel voices and dead eyes in flat faces. These shadows came around corners and jumped out of darkness from trucks and in formations. And they haunted and hunted and gathered up the children without taking the hands the children held out. These shadows were disconnected from themselves and from the children and they gained their substance from the anguish of their victims. There were no angels to stay the shadows' hands. Their little sounds...silenced...

My own little ones have grown quieter now as the darkness feels weightier. They want to be picked up, held close, their bodies limp, their speech sounds sleepy. Home is close by, its sheltering arms reaching toward them, gathering them in. They trust their Universe to keep them loved and safe.

Darkness and Light

Have you noticed
how gently darkness comes

darkness is a seductress
who seems to ask for nothing
darkness offers herself to be used
a perfect mistress for all your needs

darkness brings safety
she does not discriminate
between what should be seen
and known for what it is
and that which should remain hidden
darkness holds you close for good or ill

darkness is a secret keeper
darkness does not care who or how you choose to be
darkness does not leave you uncovered
before yourself or others

darkenss does not question
how you wrap yourself inside her
darkness will let you hide in imaginings
or help you see clearly
she offers you what you need

darkness enfolds you without consent or opposition
darkness holds a mirror in her soft hands
brings costumes for you to try on
darkness does not judge
she embroiders truth with love

but she will not tell you
what is truth

have you noticed
how the light arrives blazing and imperious
imbued with self importance
as a surgeon uses a sharpened scalpel
so light chisels the world into realities

light takes photographs of your soul
unarguably true for that moment
even when you have no need
to see or to know

light is utterly self possessed
even the plants draw in to face her
resistance is pointless

light may be soft or harsh
but you don't matter to light
she is solely about what she is
she reveals truths whether you want to know or not
and she holds you to them

sometimes we need darkness more than we need light
to see the world as we wish it to be
but this does not matter to darkness or to light
who are identical twins in opposite costumes
which they change at will
posing for one another
to give you what you feel you want or need
regardless of the truth right then

light might become a hiding place
and darkness a microscope

be grateful they are holding you
they hover close so you know
you are not alone

Shapeless and Precious Day

Have you noticed
how sometimes you are born into a shapeless day

how nothing reaches out to take you by the hand
to move you to where you want to be
an almost shy kind of a day
not brazen or clamoring for attention

these are the awakenings
when anything might be
yet nothing is

you strain to hear something anything
the sound of emptiness growing slowly
silencing anything from within

and then there is another kind of awakening
tumbling into an avalanche of obligations and desires
and the fears and the dreads of what this day may bring
what we need to feel safe withheld
crowding one another out crying to be acknowledged
and so we will fall short and we will be lost
stuck in the abundance of the chaos

still
in between the nothingness and the excess
lies our knowing deep within
just the right thing for us to choose
trusting this universe to sustain itself

that this knowing will take us by the hand
and bring us to where we can add something
to the making of a better world
because of the awesome power
of doing or not doing
just what it asks of us
this precious day

A Kind of Love

The old couple hesitates at the crosswalk
he plows ahead and she screeches
as she grabs for him calling him an old fool
but he shakes her off and moves on muttering
how she should just shut up

he looks back at her from the other side of the street
waits out of habit as she crosses to her place by his side
they move on growling softly
—whaddaya want for dinner
—no way not that again
—if ye don't like it ye should ask that Penelope you were leering at
you old lecher without a pecker of any use
he looks at her as if to make out who she is
he smiles crookedly—atta girl that's my sweetie mean as they come
—ye old coot she replies
and they lumber on
their love unexamined and enduring

Meditation

I am wandering in the no man's land of my feelings
not really lost but not really somewhere either
Happiness right over the hill and sadness down the path aways
anger gurgles in the crevasse and fear hisses in the shadows
but I don't want any of those big emotions now
grabbing insistently for my attention
making too much noise and taking up too much space

I want the quiet whispering of forbearance
the gentle hum of concern
the sweet-tart taste of melancholy
the faded pastels of gratitude

so I wait knowing that quiet subdues sounds
and rest comes after motion
and that unwelcome feelings fold back into themselves

I want a still place within now
where what comes unbidden is the sound of what is Holy
the soft voice of the Spirit
is just right for me...
now

Yesterday's Perfume

I stagger beneath
the weight of your love

wherever I am
there you are
waiting to give me what you imagine
I might need or want
or to shield me from what I do not
before I have the chance to know what that might be

it seems so perfect on the surface
each pebble brushed aside, each unevenness smoothed
leaving nothing for me to do
it passes for love
you assure me over and over again

but I sense your fear, a kind of desperation
that I might not really love you
so that by preempting any need on my part
I will not have a choice but to love you

desperation has a tell-tale scent
clinging to the skin like yesterday's perfume
stale and cloying and harsh

I need you to know that being in this prison of your making
makes me feel unseen and unknown
and feeling guilty knowing I am the cause of your pain

I want to be able to feel need and longing
because without these my world is not of my making
and I will lose myself
and we will lose each other

because I do love you
though you will not let me.

Seven Kinds of Love

They say there are seven kinds of love
so when you tell me you love me
how am I to know
which of these seven kinds you feel
and how do you know when I say I love you too
which one I feel?

when yo bring me your love
it is filled to brimming over with desire
for all you can touch of me
and thereby own
it is like staking out a piece of land
now yours forever more
or at least for the times you want to own it
and you call it love

the problem is that you do not know
that I am not there at all
that love is only what you bring to it
so I can easily let you have it
and let you call it love

what I bring you does not live in my body
it is in the pleasantness in my heart
that comes from my knowing
that you can trust me to be where you need me to be
a dependable companion on your journeys
so I get to be the giver
and the good way this makes me feel
and I call it love

so when we speak of our love
we speak of utterly different things
though each of us assumes
that the other is in the same place
and feels the same thing
like the beauty of a sunrise
or a peanut butter sandwich
and we can call it loving one another

perhaps one day we will no longer need the gentle deception
of not knowing what we sense to be true
that somewhere deep within ourselves
there are seven kinds of love

but for now I am loving
our love or our loves
or whatever this might be

Til Death Do Us Part

I want to hear your words purely
not through the fuzzy clouds of my expectations
and my hopes and my dreams but through
my holding your intentions and beliefs
your truths fully inside my being

I want to hear your words clearly
not through the haze of my fears and self-deceptions
and distortions created by stories I have told myself
embroidered with bits and pieces from lives
I have lived before you
tales and conclusions gathered
without your knowledge or consent
which cause me to lose track
of what is real and what is imagined
and who you are with me
and who I am with you

I want you to tell me that I am
all of those things I wish I were and I am not
and none of those things I am and wish I were not
I want your words to fill all the cracks and holes
so I can feel complete

and surely I want you to speak your truth to me
free of your monsters and gargoyles and spooks

then the death that will call us will not be
the death of love by attrition
or the ragged shavings of hopelessness
piling up around our being
the naked aching emptiness of feeling
unseen and unheard and unknown
stealing our breath
nor will it be the stilling of our voices by
the grinding of despair from not having been tended
when there was still time

when you say you will love and cherish me
til death do us part
I want to hear your singing to me
of the death that is the quieting of breath
and the resting of blood
and the vision of eyes beholding
the radiance of peace and
the surrender to the pure music of yet
not known love resonating in
our unyoked souls

and when I answer so will I
I want you to hear that all I have asked
of you to be for me
I yearn to be for you.

Acknowledgments

My thanks to Andy Millman, my esteemed teacher, whose encouragement and steady support allowed this work to come into being. To Chris Chambers, my editor, who guided its journey with compassion and understanding. And of course to my family, who put up with me while rolling their eyes. My deepest gratitude to you all, without whom this book would never have been.

Judith Heilizer has had a long career as a clinical psychologist. She lives in Madison, Wisconsin.

www.ingramcontent.com/pod-product-compliance
Lightning Source LLC
Chambersburg PA
CBHW032010080426
42735CB00007B/564